What Every Teacher Should Know About Multicultural and Global Education

Susan C. Brown
University of Portland

Marcella L. Kysilka
University of Central Florida

Boston   New York   San Francisco
Mexico City   Montreal   Toronto   London   Madrid   Munich   Paris
Hong Kong   Singapore   Tokyo   Cape Town   Sydney

Printed in the United States of America

10 9 8 7 6 5 4 3   11 10

Allyn & Bacon
is an imprint of

ISBN-10: 0-13-715661-8
ISBN-13: 978-0-13-715661-0

www.pearsonhighered.com

Authors' Note:

We are pleased to be presenting this booklet *What Every Teacher Should Know about Multicultural and Global Education* to preservice and practicing teachers and their instructors in teacher education institutions. We sincerely hope that this short introduction to the twin fields of multicultural education and global education will encourage educators to delve more deeply into the issues and information available about them. Reading this booklet, or even the text it is taken from (Brown and Kysilka, 2002), is just the start of a lifelong journey of commitment to providing the best education possible for all students. We wish our readers well, for the choices they make on their journeys will affect the lives of so many others.

Susan C. Brown
University of Portland

Marcella L. Kysilka
University of Central Florida

Table of Contents

INTRODUCTION

The primary concern of preservice and practicing teachers must be the students in their care. This booklet is designed for caring teachers because it is about helping these teachers to help their students succeed in the institutions that hold them captive six hours a day, five days a week, and twelve school years of a lifetime. Caring teachers surely hope that the institutions are welcoming and supportive, encouraging all students to succeed. These teachers know, however, that classroom and school environments far too often are suffocating and even threatening, discouraging students in many ways. Fortunately, the application of concepts from multicultural education and global education can provide teachers and other educators with practical possibilities, backed by theoretical foundations, for helping all their students.

Unless teachers truly understand themselves in relationship to the many cultural influences they have had over their lifetimes, they will have trouble understanding their students' cultural backgrounds and experiences, whether these are similar or different from their own. Teachers, in effect, must recognize their individual cultural identities in order to recognize and honor those of their students. Several authors discuss the difficulty of this task for White middle-class teachers, especially for White men who have never experienced personal and/or institutional discrimination (Ahlquist, 1992; Banks, 1994; Howard, 1999; Nieto, 2000). Those individuals whose ways of thinking and acting have always been considered the norm often do not recognize or do not give credit to other ways of knowing and doing. Even those individuals who have experienced discrimination in one form, for instance, might not have generalized their understanding to include acknowledgment of biases and discriminatory practices against other cultural groups such as those of class, language, religion, or ableness.

Caring preservice and practicing teachers must take the first step toward providing a welcoming and supportive learning environment for all of their students by examining their own personal cultural influences, beliefs, and attitudes. Without this necessary step, individuals cannot confront their ethnocentric biases and behaviors. They need to acknowledge and confront their deep-seated ethnocentric beliefs and biases so they can begin to develop multicultural and global perspectives. Once they have begun to develop these perspectives, teachers must in turn enable their students to live productive and contributive lives in the global society. Students themselves will need multicultural and global perspectives that give them the knowledge, skills, and attitudes to become active participants in their global world. This whole process is, of course, a monumental undertaking for even the most caring and concerned preservice and practicing teachers. The reward is the transformative knowledge, skills, and dispositions that teachers who are empowered pass on to students who then become empowered. Change can be made, and teachers can be the leaders in change making.

This booklet provides only an overview and starting point for what preservice and practicing teachers could do in a classroom, school, or community to promote multicultural and global education and to apply the concepts described. As such, it deliberately emphasizes the practical application of concepts rather than the theoretical grounding these applications are based on. Its holistic approach recognizes that all classroom elements are affected by teacher changes in behavior while appreciating that sometimes seemingly small steps are all that can be managed by overburdened preservice and practicing teachers. Small steps in the case of multicultural and global concept application can cover a lot of territory and make a huge difference if they are taken continuously and consistently.

As advocates for multicultural and global education, we the authors strongly urge that multiple perspectives be presented, analyzed, and discussed. Unless different perspectives are made explicit, many beliefs or assumptions that deeply influence attitudes and behaviors will remain unexamined. U.S. demographic studies show that the preservice and practicing teacher populations have very little of the diversity found in student populations. Bringing out alternative perspectives while discussing multicultural and global concepts with colleagues becomes even more important when other viewpoints are not there to be heard. A balanced combination of dialogue and reflection is a vital part of rich learning experiences, in our opinion.

Attempting to apply multicultural and global concepts without first examining personal beliefs, values, assumptions, and attitudes is very risky because of the emotional impact of many of the issues. Instructors and students are cautioned to establish a safe and secure classroom environment before multicultural and global education discussions that can be painful are begun. Individuals who have never confronted their own biases before will often resist, either acting out angrily or withdrawing from the conversation or even the course (Ahlquist, 1992). These discussions must not be avoided, however, since the heart and soul of the essential concepts touch also the heart and soul of humans everywhere.

As continuous discussion and reflection about multicultural and global issues causes cognitive dissonance, individuals need to find ways to cope with the emotional stress. One way is through the use of a learning log or diary in addition to the usual notebook of classroom discussions and activities. The learning log, contrary to typical professional journals, should focus on the affective aspects of learning about multicultural and global perspectives and application. Preservice and practicing teachers can gain a better understanding of their own deep-seated beliefs and values by expressing their reactions to specific issues on paper. The specific triggers and the personal reactions can be recorded for future reference. This type of learning log must be private in order for the individual to feel comfortable about revealing feelings. It should therefore be separate and apart from all other written work such as observation journals or research notes.

Even with serious self-assessment, preservice and practicing teachers will find that applying the concepts is hard work that requires the patience and dedication of a lifetime. Again, we the authors recommend strongly that all readers work in cooperative and collaborative groups. Group members can act as a support team while offering their individual perspectives on the same issues. Group members can also cheer successful efforts and, even more important, empathize and offer alternative approaches when plans or activities do not go so well. As in most teaching-learning endeavors, cooperation and collaboration keep teachers from feeling isolated and overwhelmed. Besides, this work is too valuable not to be shared with others who can benefit from participation. The reward of enriching the lives of students as well as enriching one's own personal life is worth the extra hours of thought, research, and preparation.

Terminology

Terminology changes over the years, and what was politically correct at one time might not be acceptable at another time. Terminology also changes over distance so what might be used in one place might not be used in another. Nieto (2000) suggests that terminology used to describe people be based on two criteria: (1) what the people themselves want to be called and (2) what is the most precise term. This booklet will therefore use the following:

1. African American rather than Black unless race is the specific issue;
2. American Indian or Native American;
3. Asian American;
4. European American rather than White unless race is the specific issue;
5. Latino or Hispanic;
6. People of color as a collective term for people of African American, Latino, Asian American, and American Indian backgrounds rather than non-Whites or minorities;
7. United States rather than America for the country; United States or U.S. instead of American.

In cases where a specific group within these larger categories is being discussed, that term will be used. For example, Puerto Rican or Cuban American will be chosen over Latino or Hispanic if either of those more specific groups is discussed.

The terms "culture" and "cultural group" have different definitions depending upon the various authors' viewpoints. The definition of culture given by Nieto (2000) is used in this text:

> Culture consists of the values, traditions, social and political relationships, and worldview created, shared, and transformed by a group of people bound together by a common history, geographic location, language, social class, and/or religion, and how these are transformed by those who share them. (p. 138)

Thus, a cultural group is a group of people who share a common culture. In this booklet, the following cultural groups and their issues are discussed: race/ethnicity, class, religion, gender, sexual orientation, ableness, age, geographic location, and nationality.

In this booklet, race and ethnicity are grouped together for the discussion of issues, although they are not synonymous terms. Race does not have biological or genetic meaning, but historically the concept of race has been used to categorize people for purposes of discrimination and oppression. Like race, ethnicity has served as a form of group identification. An ethnic group as defined by Banks (1994) is "an involuntary collectivity of people with a shared feeling of common identity, a sense of peoplehood, and a shared sense of interdependence of fate" (p. 71). Although membership in an ethnic group is involuntary, individual identification with the group is optional. Federal and state forms use combinations of racial, ethnic, and linguistic classifications to identify individuals for a variety of purposes including funding, but any forced labeling of people becomes problematic at best. The richness of cultural diversity in the United States cannot be captured in little boxes. Yet the terms must be considered precisely because of their historical, political, social, and economic implications.

PART ONE
Understanding Essential Multicultural and Global Concepts

The twenty-first century will be one of increasing diversity among the peoples of the United States. People of color, onc-fourth of the population in 1990, will soon be one-third of the population. In two states, California and Texas, and in many of the major cities, students of color are over half of the public school population.

The immigrant population, from as geographically and culturally diverse groups as Hispanics, Filipinos, Vietnamese, and Russians, will continue to grow in the twenty-first century. The majority of these immigrants are school-aged children, some with little or no experience with schooling.

Linguistic diversity is also increasing in the United States. Although English continues to be the language of economic and social advance, 14 percent of the school population speaks another language at home. In many schools today, over fifty different languages are spoken by students. For instance, students in one high school in Orange County, Florida, have fifty-two different Latino, Asian, and Eastern European first languages. In addition, numerous other schoolchildren speak some form of dialect or nonstandard English.

Another increasing area of diversity is class as the U.S. population continues to show a widening disparity between the rich and the poor. According to federal government standards, about 20 percent of the population lives below the poverty line. Families in poverty are often headed by single parents, usually women, and have school-aged children.

From these statistics and others, including those for religion and exceptionality, comes the obvious prediction that teachers will continue to work with students of ever-increasing diversity. Yet the teacher population at the turn of twenty-first century is still primarily European American, middle class, Christian, and female. Efforts to attract qualified people from diverse ethnic and racial backgrounds into teaching have met with limited success. Thus the large majority of teachers, in the beginning of the twenty-first century at least, do not have the same cultural heritage and experiences as a large percentage of their students. How teachers work in classrooms, schools, and communities to teach, honor, and empower all students to be successful is the essence of multicultural and global education as applied in teachers' lives.

Essential Multicultural and Global Concepts

Controversy has surrounded the concepts of multiculturalism and multicultural education from the start (de Anda, 1997; Sleeter & McLaren, 1995). Many people, including educators like Ravitch (1990), see any approach that emphasizes individual and group differences as being divisive. Others are worried that multiculturalism ultimately means cultural relativism, the acceptance of all beliefs and values as equal. While some wonder what the fuss is all about since there are laws to protect individuals against discrimination, others see laws such as affirmative action legislature as a chance for less-qualified individuals to take away positions from those who rightfully earned them. On the other hand, the radical left critics, such as Giroux (1996), complain that multicultural education is more interested in obtaining justice for students in schools than in confronting the larger societal structure and institutions that oppress groups.

Controversial elements of multicultural education are initially divisive, especially when individuals are forced to confront their own biases and prejudices. Yet no thoughtful educator can ignore the weight of statistics about the students we fail to educate in our school systems. Authors such as Kozol

(1991) and Delpit (1995) remind us that student populations that are poor, live in urban settings, have limited English proficiency, and belong to cultural groups of color have high percentages of academic failure. If advocates of multicultural education see the application of its principles as a hopeful way to reach all schoolchildren, then teachers have an obligation to investigate what multicultural education has to offer them.

Global education has had a very different reception from multicultural education. For the most part, global education has been ignored until the contextual circumstances of a school, district, or state have forced some sort of reluctant acknowledgment of its necessity (Diaz, Massialas, & Xanthopoulos, 1999; Merryfield, Jarchow, & Pickert, 1997). Although economic fears drive much of this concern, the reality of global interdependence confronts us in daily issues and events such as global warming predictions and international terrorism. As the new millennium starts, the global economy and the international communication network are forcing educators and policymakers alike to reevaluate their positions.

Being a part of the economically and politically powerful United States has affected the viewpoints of many Americans towards other countries and continents. Because of their privileged positions as U.S. citizens, they tend to be insular and poorly informed about issues elsewhere. In a sense, they have attitudes found commonly in a dominant cultural group: "It's their problem; let them solve it." The lack of knowledge and understanding about realities in other parts of the world give U.S. citizens, especially those who have not lived or traveled extensively in other countries, less chance for comparisons and contrasts and less possibility of seeing other perspectives. This insular approach also leads some critics to feel that it is somehow un-American to find fault in the international policies and practices of U.S. companies and the government. Stressing global perspectives in the classroom, however, does not lead to a diminishing of national pride but a heightening awareness of citizen duties, responsibilities, and positive global attitudes (Diaz et al., 1999). Teachers need to be aware of international concerns and controversies, especially those involving the United States, so they can act as informed citizens and participants in the global society.

Defining Multicultural Education

Multicultural Education Approaches

Multicultural education has taken several forms over the last thirty or forty years. In the 1960s three different approaches emerged, according to Sleeter and Grant (1988). The first was teaching the exceptional and the culturally different. This was primarily seen as a way to help students of color, students in poverty, students with limited English proficiency, and students who had special educational needs succeed in mainstream education. The second was the human relations approach, an attempt to help people with differing backgrounds—especially race, gender, and ableness—communicate and work together better. The third was the single group studies, especially ethnic and women's studies, which tried to raise consciousness about that group's oppression and to take social action.

By the 1970s, two more approaches were emerging. The first one, multicultural education, is described by Sleeter and Grant (1988) as an approach that "links race, language, culture, gender, handicap, and, to a lesser extent, social class, working toward making the entire school celebrate human diversity and equal opportunity" (p. 28). The second approach, education that is multicultural and social reconstructionist, extends the multicultural education approach to social action and the restructuring of teaching-learning contexts and society itself. This approach emphasizes the process and context as well as the

4

content, and leads students to be decision makers and change makers for social good.

Think and Act
- Make a note of your first awareness of the term "multicultural education." Was it in public school, university, teacher training, or in practice?
- Describe your first impressions of multicultural education. Did you relate it to your personal life and/or your teaching? Did you relate it to a particular cultural group, a specific content, an experience, and/or a philosophy?
- Research past issues of your local newspaper for mention of the terms "multicultural," "multiculturalism," and "diversity." How are the terms used? In what contexts?

Multicultural Education as a Process
Although Sleeter and Grant's (1988) terminology for this approach, "education that is multicultural and social reconstructivist," has not been adopted by most authors in the field, the concept of change making or transformation is basic to most definitions. In this booklet, multicultural education is seen as a combination of definitions by Geneva Gay (1994) and Sonia Nieto (2000). Gay (1994) sees multicultural education as

> the policies, programs, and practices employed in schools to celebrate cultural diversity. It builds on the assumption that teaching and learning are invariably cultural processes. Since schools are composed of students and teachers from a wide variety of cultural backgrounds, the best way for the educational process to be most effective for the greatest number of students is for it to be multicultural. (p. 3)

Although this definition sounds as if any policy, program, or practice used to mention diversity would qualify as multicultural education, Gay is very careful to define "celebrate" as incorporating the appropriate knowledge, skills, attitudes, and behavior needed. Events such as international festivals are often considered community celebrations, but they would not fit Gay's definition of celebrating cultural diversity in the truest sense.

Nieto's (2000) definition puts more emphasis than Gay's on the dynamic process component of multicultural education. In her text, Affirming Diversity, Nieto (2000) states:

> Multicultural education is a process of comprehensive school reform and basic education for all students. It challenges and rejects racism and other forms of discrimination in schools and society and accepts and affirms the pluralism (ethnic, racial, linguistic, religious, economic, and gender, among others) that students, their communities, and teachers reflect. Multicultural education permeates the schools' curriculum and instructional strategies, as well as the interactions among teachers, students, and families, and the very way that schools conceptualize the nature of teaching and learning. Because it uses critical pedagogy as its underlying philosophy and focuses on knowledge, reflection, and action (praxis) as the basis for social change, multicultural education promotes the democratic principles of social justice. (p. 305)

Although sexual orientation, age, and ableness are not explicitly stated, these cultural groups must also be included. Nieto's definition expects teachers, students, and other participants in multicultural education to play active roles in the ongoing process of promoting social justice. Also stressed is the complete involvement of every part in the educational system.

Multicultural education that calls for social action is similar to critical pedagogy in that "both refer to a particular ethico-political attitude or ideological stance that one constructs in order to confront and engage the world critically and challenge power relations" (Sleeter & McLaren, 1995, p. 7). Teachers who support these positions are not just actively working toward human rights, equality of opportunity, and so forth in their classrooms. They become "cultural workers" for social justice in that their context goes beyond the classrooms to schools and other public arenas such as community centers and social services (Freire, 1998; Sleeter & McLaren, 1995).

Recognizing multicultural education as a dynamic process that changes the teaching-learning contexts leads to the acknowledgment of the interaction of critical elements in the classroom, the school, and the community. The classroom elements are the teacher, the students, the classroom environment, the curriculum, the instruction, and the assessment. Critical elements beyond the classroom are the school and the community. The outcome of multicultural education would be students having the knowledge, skills, attitudes, and behaviors to be active participants for a democratic and just society.

Think and Act
- What do you remember from your own schooling about issues related to multicultural education? Share in a group your most vivid impressions and analyze their effects.
- Why have many teachers centered on celebrating special cultural events as their approach to multicultural education? Why are topics like racism and sexism avoided or minimized?
- Describe what Nieto (2000) means by a process as it relates to you and your teaching. Where do you see yourself in this process now? Five years from now?

Defining Global Education

Global Education Content

Global education, sometimes associated with but distinct from multicultural education, can be seen as having multicultural concepts applied to the world community and emphasizing the planet, its natural resources, and all interconnections. The Hanvey (1976) model includes five interdisciplinary dimensions. The first, perspective consciousness, includes an awareness of and appreciation for other viewpoints of the world. The second, state of the planet awareness, emphasizes global issues and events. The third, cross-cultural awareness, is an understanding of world cultures, especially in light of similarities and differences. The fourth, systemic awareness, deals with the nature of global systems and their patterns of interrelationships and interdependence. The fifth, options for participation, presents possibilities for participating in local, national, and international settings.

Although earlier explanations of content for global education were expressed more as intellectual understandings (Hanvey, 1976; Kniep, 1986), more recent approaches have included social action as well as social thought and debate. Merryfield and colleagues' (1997) content list, for example, contains eight general elements: human beliefs and values, global systems, global issues and problems, global history, cross-cultural understanding and interaction, awareness of human choices, development of analytical and evaluative skills, and strategies for participation and involvement. Educators such as Kirkwood (1990), who implemented global education in Dade County, FL, would agree with viewing global education as an agent for social action and change.

Think and Act

- Make a note of your first awareness of the term "global education." Was it in public school, university, teacher training, or in practice?
- Describe your first impressions of global education. Did you relate it to your personal life and/or your teaching? Did you relate it to a particular national group or groups, a specific content, an experience and/or a philosophy?
- Research past issues of your local newspaper for mention of the terms "global education," and "global competition," and "global village." How are the terms used? In what contexts?

Global Education as a Process

As global education has matured over the years, the definitions have also been refined. An early definition of global education used by the National Council for the Social Studies (NCSS, 1982) is:

> Global education is an effort to cultivate in young people a perspective of the world which emphasizes the interconnections among cultures, species, and the planet. The purpose of global education is to develop in youth the knowledge, skills, and attitudes needed to live effectively in a world possessing limited natural resources and characterized by ethnic diversity, cultural pluralism, and increasing interdependence. (pp. 1–2)

Merryfield's 1994 definition, although very similar, differs in crucial ways:

> Global education develops the knowledge, skills, and attitudes that are necessary for decision-making and effective participation in a world characterized by interconnectedness, cultural pluralism, and increasing competition for resources. (p. 4)

Merryfield's substitution of "decision-making and effective participation" for "living effectively" gives a clearer image of a proactive person. The addition of the element of economic competition for the limited world resources and markets reflects the more modern concerns of the twenty-first century.

Teachers advocating global education would think in terms of the multicultural global village and its problems, rather than considering only the multicultural community of the immediate or national environment. Like multicultural education, however, global education is also seen as a process that transforms. Teachers who support global education also wish to enlighten and empower students for the social good.

Think and Act
- What do you remember from your own schooling about issues related to global education? Share in a group your most vivid impressions and analyze their effects.
- Why have many teachers centered on concepts and related activities like pollution and recycling? Why isn't there more emphasis on dangers of international conglomerates, for instance?
- Describe what is meant by "a world characterized by cultural pluralism, interconnectedness, and international economic competition" as it relates to you and your teaching now and five years from now.

Combining Multicultural and Global Education

As can be seen from the earlier discussions, multicultural education and global education have many commonalties but different emphases. Both involve a process whereby individuals develop knowledge, skills, attitudes, and behaviors for - participating effectively in a culturally diverse society. While multicultural education stresses individuals and cultural groups within their local and national society, global education emphasizes world problems and interconnections within the global context. When combined, multicultural education and global education can be seen as two parts of the same theme of how individuals, groups, and institutions can work together to build a better world locally, nationally, and internationally (Brown, 1993).

The resulting definition for multicultural and global education used in this booklet is the following:

> Multicultural and global education can be seen as the educational process of acquiring certain knowledge, skills, and values to participate actively in a complex, pluralistic, and interconnected world society and to work together for change in individuals and institutions in order to make that world society more just and humane.

This definition includes student preparation to become knowledgeable, caring, and active citizens. Implied is the need to develop and practice the skills of citizenship. The focus is not only on the diversity of individuals and cultural groups but also on the interconnectedness of all individuals and groups and the need to work together for solving the world's problems.

Combining the Major Concepts of
Multicultural and Global Education

In 1984, Donna Cole discussed common connections between multicultural education and global education that she could anticipate leading to a merger of "multiculturalized global education" (p. 153). Using Cole's ideas combined with references from multicultural education and global education, Brown (1993) listed five categories, which are discussed in the sections below.

> Understanding of social living in groups
> Understanding of the "other"
> Understanding of interrelatedness and interdependence
> Development of skills in living with diversity
> Adjustment to changes for the future

Social Living in Groups

This concept involves understanding oneself and how one fits into cultural groups and into larger macrocultures, such as the United States and Earth. Each person needs to understand himself or herself as an individual, a member of various cultural groups, and a member of humanity. One way to see this conceptually is to imagine each individual as a whole pie shape divided into three equal parts. The first third is composed of individual characteristics—what makes that person unique. The second third is composed of cultural group characteristics—what makes that person part of the specific culture or cultures relevant in that particular situation. The last third is composed of human characteristics—what makes that person part of humanity.

Keeping all three parts of any individual's characteristics in balance is an important part of the combined multicultural and global education. A heavy emphasis on any one of the parts affects the other two parts. If teachers look at only the individual characteristics of their students, the students' memberships in cultural groups might be ignored. For instance, one European American middle school male teacher demanded that a young Latino being disciplined look at him directly: "Look me in the eye. A man looks a man in the eye!" (Brown, personal experience). The teacher focused only on the individual and ignored, or was ignorant of, any possible differences in cultural behaviors. If that student's Latino relatives had taught him to stare at the ground to show his humility and lower status when being disciplined, for the student not to do that would be, in effect, an insult to the teacher according to his culture. Such cultural mismatches can leave students bewildered, embarrassed, or frustrated.

In an attempt to avoid uncomfortable issues, some European American teachers naively state that they see every student as an individual, not as a member of a race. According to Nieto (2000), these teachers are like most Whites, who have the advantage of seeing themselves as individuals—"an opportunity not generally afforded to those from dominated groups" (p. 79). In this case, the overemphasis on the individual reduces the importance of the cultural group of race, minimizing or ignoring real problems such as personal and institutional racism.

An overemphasis on the specific cultural group of an individual also affects the other two parts. When others acknowledge only the race or the religion of an outsider person, they are ignoring that person's individual characteristics and human characteristics. In this form, such an emphasis becomes the basis for "isms" such as racism and sexism. The Ku Klux Klan and neo-Nazi groups, for instance, foster extreme hatred by whipping up emotions around one salient group characteristic such as skin color. Groups themselves can overemphasize the group, forcing members to give up individual choices different from the group or friendships with others outside the group. Some religious groups like the Amish might not directly target other religions, but unity is achieved at the price of submitting to the group will. In the case of cults, submission is to the leaders as ultimate authorities.

Ethnic studies provide the positive benefits of supplementing cultural history and information too often lacking in the middle-class European American Christian curriculum that dominates most U.S. schools. One potential danger, however, is that an extreme emphasis on ethnicity could ignore individual differences within the group or ignore the commonalties found in humans. Examination of multicultural issues through the study of various cultural groups contains the same risks, since generalizations about groups can easily lead into stereotypes. For example, in interactions like the one mentioned above between the European American teacher and the Latino student, a rigid expectation that every European American man would demand eye-to-eye contact or that every Latino boy would feel conflict and embarrassment would be stereotyping both persons even if their respective cultural groups had tendencies to act in certain predictable ways. In any interaction, the individuals must be considered as well as their cultural groups.

Finally, an overemphasis on the similarities of people as humans can adversely affect the acceptance of individual and group characteristics of a person. Those people who wish to see multicultural and global education as only an acknowledgment of similarities between individuals and groups ignore the multitude of differences within the human race, both as individuals and as cultural groups. Yet the differences are at the center of cultural conflicts. Human history is full of such conflicts, whether caused by race, religion, class, or combinations of these and others. Personal biases, group discrimination, and institutional oppression can be witnessed throughout the world, whether "ethnic cleansing" as in Bosnia, homophobic murders as in the United

States, or economic domination of "have not" countries by multinational corporations.

The strong emphasis put on commonalties of humans might leave individuals and groups isolated and frustrated because they do not match the norm model of the dominant society. Certainly their experiences of discrimination in the United States tell children and adults that females are not males, and people of color are not White, Jewish are not Christian, and so forth. Kim, a White student teacher, was heard comforting a Black second-grade girl in a predominantly White class. The girl had just said that nobody liked her because she was Black. The student teacher's comment was "It's because you're new here and the other children don't know you. I remember when I was new in school...." The student teacher's attempt to comfort the little girl ignored the child's race and stressed only the similarities of the human experience of being in a new social situation. In a sense, she treated the girl's blackness as nothing, not worth bothering about, instead of acknowledging two crucial points: the reality of possible racism and the richness of diverse cultural heritages.

Think and Act
- Describe briefly a childhood incident (one that you are willing to share) when you were discriminated against because of your membership in a cultural group. Explain your feelings at the time of the incident. Looking back, how do you feel now?
- Observe a group of students talking among themselves. Note the power relationships. Who dominates and is listened to? Who is ignored or excluded?
- Share stories told by children about acts of discrimination. Compare and contrast these stories to your own.

The "Other"

The combined multicultural and global education concept emphasizes multiple perspectives. If every individual is unique, carrying a unique combination of individual, group, and human characteristics that is "self," then each person's perspective or worldview is also unique. In dealing with ethnic identity issues, the difficulty comes in recognizing other perspectives as valid while maintaining a positive attitude and self-esteem about one's own ethnicity. Teachers will probably find this concept the most challenging, since it touches many core beliefs and values. Yet teachers and students must be open to other perspectives for any multicultural and global learning to happen.

An initial step to understanding can be gained by being aware of the growth process necessary. Banks (1991) describes stages that individuals can experience in his typology of ethnic identifications: Stage 1, ethnic psychological captivity; Stage 2, ethnic encapsulation; Stage 3, ethnic identity clarification; Stage 4, biethnicity; Stage 5, multiethnicity and reflective nationalism; and Stage 6, globalism and global competency. Banks suggests that these stages are developmental, although not strictly sequential, and that the stages are not distinctly separated.

The first two stages have serious negative implications. Stage 1, ethnic psychological captivity, describes the individuals who have low self-esteem and shame about their ethnicity as a result of internalizing the negative beliefs and ideologies about that ethnicity that are found in the dominant society. This would be typical of Blacks, for instance, who have internalized the White message of the lighter the skin, the better. Stage 2, ethnic encapsulation, describes the individuals who see only their ethnic position or viewpoint as the right or superior one as a result of living and working primarily within their own community and accepting the societal myths about their ethnic superiority. This would be typical of Whites who have not been forced to examine their privileged position in U.S. society or who have felt so threatened by confrontation with another ethnic group that they have reacted negatively.

Stage 3 of the typology by Banks (1991), ethnic identity clarification, is the beginning of a positive approach to ethnicity. It describes the individuals who have positive self-acceptance of their own ethnicity and are ready to respond positively to other ethnic groups. Stage 4, biethnicity, describes the individuals who are bicultural with positive ethnic identities and the skills to function successfully in two cultures. Stage 5, multiethnicity and reflective nationalism, describes the individuals who are able to function effectively within several ethnic and cultural groups. This stage, according to Banks (1991), represents "the idealized goal for citizenship identity within an ethnically pluralistic nation" (p. 66). As such, the fifth stage is the desired outcome of multicultural education.

Stage 6, globalism and global competency, describes the individuals who have achieved the highest level by being able to function effectively in ethnic cultures nationally and internationally. According to Banks (1991), these individuals "have internalized universalistic ethical values and principles of humankind and have the skills, competencies, and commitments needed to act on these values" (p. 66). This sixth stage represents the desired outcome of multicultural and global education and the goal of this booklet.

Although the typology by Banks (1991) refers specifically to ethnic identity, similar stages can be found with other cultural identifications. Sexual orientation, for instance, becomes extremely sensitive as children reach puberty. While adolescents of color may have special difficulties because of racist issues in the dominant society, all adolescents face struggles with finding their identities, including their sexuality (Santrock, 2001). Therefore, it is very understandable why middle school becomes the place for serious sexual harassment and why boys and girls who think they are gay, lesbian, bisexual, or transsexual feel so much at risk. Without a supportive environment at home and in school, they internalize the homophobic messages their peers and adults send.

Tied with multiple perspectives is the understanding of knowledge as a construction process, one of Banks's (1997) dimensions of multicultural education. Historical data and explanations in textbooks, for instance, can be seen as selected information reflecting the viewpoint of the dominant culture instead of as objective, accurate reports of past times and events. When viewed in this manner, all sources of information become open to examination for omissions, distortions, and biases. Multiple perspectives bring in the voices not heard when historical material has been processed through ethnocentric filters by the winners of any cultural conflicts.

Multiple perspectives affect cultural, national, and international viewpoints as well as individual ones. The concentration on Western civilization in high schools and universities to the marginalization or exclusion of world cultures has left U.S. students ignorant of much of the world's rich history. Presenting these from multiple perspectives adds a richness and wholeness not seen in the Eurocentric perspectives of most history textbooks in the United States. Global history or global studies, a content dimension of global education (Kniep, 1986; Merryfield et al., 1997), reminds teachers of global systems, global interconnectedness and interdependence, and global problems and issues in the past, present, and future. Unfortunately, the courses are too often taught from a European American perspective by teachers who are woefully lacking in world history and world studies content knowledge.

Think and Act

- Choose a recent local or TV event known by you and several others. Each person jot down details of what happened. Compare results.
- Use a newspaper account of some educational issue as a starter. Put down as many perspectives as you can. Discuss who might hold each perspective and why.
- Make a collection of international news stories from your local newspaper. Discuss the perspectives presented. Note what American interests are revealed. Why are these particular stories given space in the newspaper?

Interrelatedness and Interdependence

This aspect of multicultural and global education is particularly important in the information age. In the past few years, as the concept of a global village has become more of a reality to students and teachers everywhere, global education as a discipline has gained momentum and greater recognition, although multicultural education is still more widespread (Merryfield et al., 1997). Instant access to information about these individuals and institutions, even instant access to the people and groups themselves, has brought about a realization that isolation from the world and its problems is virtually impossible. Interrelatedness, or interconnectedness as used in much of global education literature, and interdependence are certainly realities as well as global concepts for the twenty-first century.

Global systems, according to Kniep (1986) and Merryfield and colleagues (1997), include economic, political, technological, and ecological elements and the ways they are interconnected and interdependent; a change in one part affects other parts. For instance, an example witnessed and explained to one of the authors involved a small settlement of Brazilian Indians. Years earlier a European-owned manufacturing plant built in the upper Amazon region attracted many impoverished people, some walking two hours each way to earn very low wages. Then in the early 1990s, a cruise line arranged with the settlement leaders to allow the passengers a tour of the village and its homes. The tourists with their dollars disrupted the village patterns again, making it more profitable for the villagers to sell handmade goods or to beg than to walk to work. Both the manufacturing plant and the cruise line provided much-needed wages and, in the case of the cruise line at least, extra funds for building and supplying an elementary school. Yet the two international corporations destroyed the traditional way of life without replacing it with a stable, self-sufficient economy. A small village, international corporations, several countries and their governments, and citizens from a multitude of nations all became interconnected and interdependent, creating one example of a global problem.

Think and Act
- Jot down two or three personal ties to people and organizations outside of your country. How were the ties established? How are they maintained? What purpose do they have in your life?
- Think of a recent world event that has had an impact on your life. Describe the circumstances and your reaction.

Living with Diversity
As the world becomes more and more interconnected and interdependent, the skills of working cooperatively with others for solutions to local, national, and international global problems become more and more important. At the local level, corporations

and institutions have become more service oriented, demanding of their employees better interpersonal skills to deal with suppliers and customers. Businesses also expect the employees to be able to work on teams within the company to problem solve. As businesses expand nationally and internationally, executives are learning that their employees must have appropriate skills for living and working with diverse people. In international situations, company representatives stationed in foreign countries have found that corporate success often depends more upon the expatriate manager's personal skills of empathy, ability to remain nonjudgmental, and tolerance for ambiguity rather than his or her technical and managerial skills (Gregersen & Black, 1990; Hall & Gudykunst, 1989).

The Brazilian story highlights the question of responsibility for global problems and issues. The corporations were not the only participants in disrupting the village way of life. People who demanded cheaper goods and people who paid to see the Amazon and its inhabitants must also take responsibility. The governments that allowed the exploitation of labor must also be held responsible. Global problems and global issues then become everyone's responsibility. Learning about these concerns and what individuals can do is an initial step toward bringing about change.

Think and Act
- Describe briefly a childhood incident (one that you are willing to share) when you overcame a misunderstanding related to differences in cultural backgrounds. What responsibility did each person take for clearing up the misunderstanding?
- Investigate one of several issues associated with huge cruise ships: influx of foreign capital, pollution of the oceans, disruption of traditional ways and livelihoods,

redistribution of land, etc. What perspectives do the various stakeholders take?
- Write letters to cruise lines or international entertainment groups such as Club Med about their policies and practices toward indigenous peoples in impoverished areas. Ask how they contribute to the welfare of the communities other than through salaries.

Changes for the Future

Adjustment to changes must be seen as active preparation for the future rather than a passive acceptance of what is to come. Part of this active participation is the use of knowledge and skills to work toward solutions to local, national, and international problems and issues. This combines the personal need to be flexible and open to multiple perspectives with the ability to act for social justice. Multicultural and global education is a positive approach and a process empowering students now for present and future action.

Think and Act

- Name one action you have taken outside the classroom for social justice. It can be something in your personal life such as a stand against racist or sexist jokes or a position in your professional life such as membership to an organization promoting multicultural or global concepts. Why did you do this? What type of personal courage did it take?
- Prepare and role play scenarios from these personal experiences of you and your teammates. Ask the audience to provide a variety of endings.

Applying Multicultural and Global
Education in the Classroom

The six applications below come from the multicultural and global education concepts just discussed. If teachers truly support multicultural and global education, in our opinion, teachers must accept both the concepts and the process of empowering students. Belief in multicultural and global education must become part of teachers' core values and beliefs system. If the belief is not internalized, teachers will only bring superficial aspects of multicultural and global education into their classrooms. They will be unable to bring the kind of multicultural and global education that empowers students to participate actively as global citizens.

> Diversity must be celebrated.
> Human rights must be honored.
> Multiple perspectives must be sought.
> Interconnectedness and interdependence must be developed.
> Co-responsibility must be practiced.
> The global society must be experienced.

Diversity
Diversity of every sort makes up our planet Earth, providing infinite variety in so many ways. The richness of that diversity is something to enjoy, treasure, and protect. In a similar way, diversity of humans and human characteristics fills the classroom. The wide variety found in even a small handful of students offers exciting possibilities to the teacher who knows how to take advantage of these differences. In multicultural and global education, the diversity of humans is seen as a richness to be enjoyed, treasured, and protected. Teachers and students must not see diversity as a problem. The challenge is not the diversity itself

but tapping into the diversity in a positive way. Given the global village of today with its interconnectedness and interdependence, students need regular and positive experiences with as many types of diversity as possible. Such experiences, with the guidance of the teacher, will help them to develop the lifelong skills needed to be a proactive citizen in the global society. Not providing students with tools to enjoy and benefit from diversity is a serious neglect on the part of any teacher.

Think and Act
- Why might a teacher be unwilling to see diversity as something to celebrate?
- Jot down three types of diversity that seem the most challenging in a classroom. Give a reason for each choice. Compare your results with two or three others.
- Attend an event or exhibit that highlights types of diversity in your community. Look beyond ethnic and racial diversity for examples.

Human Rights
Lynch (1992) advocates that multicultural and global education should start with human rights at its core. In the classroom, human rights must certainly be a main emphasis. Each student must feel safe, secure, and wanted as a member of the class. All students need to learn how to work with one another without resorting to bullying, name calling, or any painful tactics. For teachers, honoring human rights means not exploiting the power and position by using sarcasm or any other form of belittling. Beyond avoiding blatant behavior, however, is the subtler positive behavior of affirming students and their diverse cultural heritages and experiences.

In many U.S. schools, student harassment of other students is a common occurrence. Corridors and cafeterias have become hostile places for the targeted individuals or groups. Teachers and administrators have an obligation to prevent such behavior from continuing and to punish those who persist. Ignoring verbal and physical threats creates tolerance for discrimination, thereby destroying the foundations for any application of multicultural and global education. Schools and communities can work together to reduce racism, sexism, and classism in the schools. Programs such as those that stress conflict resolution can help students find alternatives to violence. Other programs—such as diversity training—can increase understanding and appreciation of cultural differences among all school members.

Nationally and internationally, human rights issues can be explored using a variety of sources including the Internet. For instance, the Universal Declaration of Human Rights, adopted by the United Nations in 1948, and the Convention on the Rights of a Child, ratified in 1989 by all United Nations members except Somalia and the United States, can be studied. Of interest to older students can be the reasons given by the United States for not ratifying the latter. UNICEF information about the living and working conditions of women and children around the world can be found on numerous Internet sites, including www.unicef.org/aclabor

---

Think and Act

•   Remember an incident of name calling when you were a student. How did you feel? How did the teacher act? From each child's perspective, was the incident resolved successfully? From your adult perspective now, what should a teacher have done?

- Call the local school board to see what sort of diversity training is provided in the district for administrators, teachers, and staff. Ask for copies of the literature used.
- Check Internet sites either women's rights or children's rights information. Research a particular issue such as sweatshops.

Multiple Perspectives

The acceptance of diversity of humans as a richness means also the acceptance of different ways of looking at the world, for each human in his or her uniqueness looks at the world through a unique perspective. Teachers have the huge responsibility of seeing and searching out other perspectives while helping students to do the same. They must model the openness and flexibility needed for empathizing with others. They must be able to walk in another's moccasins, truly understanding where that person is situated in the world. This openness and flexibility must be for their own students first, then for the other voices not ordinarily heard. Teachers and students together must actively seek out places and spaces in the critical classroom elements described later where one viewpoint only is represented and where other viewpoints are missing.

Think and Act
- How does the saying "walk in another's moccasins" demonstrate a universal idea while portraying specific American Indian cultures? Research the origin of this saying.
- The saying is often stated as "walk a mile in another man's moccasins." What perspective does "a mile" imply? How do you know that this is an inaccurate perspective for the

saying? What perspective does "man's" imply? What kind of research would be necessary to check the accuracy of this part?
• Discuss the full inclusion issue from the different perspectives of the full inclusion child, the other children, the teacher, and the parents.

Interconnectedness and Interdependence
The Internet has brought the world into the classroom and the classroom into the world in a very obvious way. Before the Internet, however, forces around the world daily affected the lives of teachers and students, either directly or indirectly. When OPEC decided to restrict the quantity of petroleum sold in the world, the cost of gas for cars went up in the United States. Higher gas prices made a greater demand for small- and medium-sized cars. When U.S.-based companies found new sources of cheap labor in countries such as Indonesia and China, less expensive clothing flooded the market. Companies continue to justify low wages to their workers, in the United States or elsewhere, by claiming international competition. Thousands and perhaps millions of examples can be found as more economic, social, and political ties are made every day.

In the classroom, teachers need to point out the fast-growing international as well as national aspects of students' own lives. Using the community's resources, students can make links to other people and places. Companies with national and international branches, families with relatives in other cities and countries, and social organizations with national and international affiliations are among the possibilities. Having students establish their own interconnected webs gives them realistic experiences and opportunities to practice skills for their global world.

Classes can also explore the ecological issues within the concept of interconnectedness. For example, the change in oceanic ecosystems caused by the dumping of ballast waters from tankers can be a research area. Land use can include the ongoing arguments about the destruction of forests such as the Amazon, which can be investigated. Studying the cycle of deforestation, and cultivation leading to depletion of the already poor soil and the probable creation of deserts can trigger questions about the livelihoods of poor Brazilians and the involvement of multinational companies.

Think and Act
- Have students work out the different possibilities for connections with other classmates. Suggestions include classes, cafeteria, sports, extracurricular clubs, transportation to school, friends outside school, neighbors, and relatives.
- Refer back to your notes about personal ties to people and organizations outside of your country. How can these be shared with your students? What benefits can you see for both groups of people?
- Select a water or land use issue that is debated globally. Present several positions on the issue, including those of the multinational companies and the indigenous peoples.
- Investigate a local water or land use issue and positions presented in the local newspapers and media.

Co-Responsibility
"If you are not part of the solution, you are part of the problem." Issues of racism, sexism, and classism, for example, are so complex and so buried in individuals and institutions that

wholesale reform is needed to correct the injustices. For example, White teachers who say that they do not need multiculturalism in their classroom because they do not have any children of color have not yet acknowledged the position of favor they and their students have had by being White. They have also ignored all the other concerns that multicultural and global education addresses: ethnicity, class, gender, sexual orientation, and so on. These teachers, and others like them from all ethnic and cultural groups, need extensive, in-depth education to overcome their ignorance about these concepts and their reluctance to take responsibility for their application.

Teachers can and must be part of the solution by first being open to personal and professional growth and change. With growth and change, they can become change makers themselves, helping their students in turn to become change makers. Teachers and students everywhere have to work at the personal and institutional levels to overcome discrimination of any kind. Practice begins in the classroom where the teacher and students together learn about multicultural and global concepts and take the responsibility to apply them in their daily lives.

Think and Act
- How have you dealt with discriminatory comments or jokes in the past?
- What part of your class rules deals with co-responsibility to overcome discrimination of any kind? How is that made clear to the students?
- What does taking a passive role in solving multicultural and global problems imply?

Global Society

As the world is brought into the classroom, the students must go out into the world. Teachers have a responsibility to help their students prepare for the world in as many ways as possible. Part of this responsibility is to help students be actors rather than spectators in their world. Projects that involve change in local conditions, for instance, are ways to give students voices outside the classroom. This belief is expressed in "Think globally, act locally," with the understanding that action comes after reflective consideration. Students need to practice the skills of advocacy now in a safe context so that they will be able to use the skills throughout life.

Skills for a global society include appropriate application of the five concepts just discussed. Celebrating diversity, for instance, is a meaningless phrase unless it can be applied in students' lives. Skills for celebrating diversity include the ability to be open to other viewpoints and to withhold judgment until all perspectives are sought and examined. Other skills needed for a global society include being flexible and willing to accept change. Acceptance of change is not enough, however, because only empowered global citizens can participate in bringing about change.

The information age is forcing changes of all sorts at an ever-increasing pace. One crucial change in the past few years, the access to information through technology, has so radically affected human lives worldwide that individuals and institutions without technology are the "have-nots" of the twenty-first century. Teachers who are not computer literate are at risk because they cannot assist their students in developing essential skills of information collecting, sorting, and applying. Students with fewer opportunities to use computers in their classrooms and homes will be at a disadvantage in many ways, especially economically since virtually every business in the United States now depends upon computer-stored and manipulated information. Teachers have an obligation, therefore, to keep up with technological changes and to facilitate their students' learning in these areas. They also have an obligation to fight for the resources necessary to supply their students with these crucial tools.

Change-making skills include the ability to think critically and creatively; the ability to work collaboratively on complex, persistent human problems; and the ability to carry out long-term goals through action steps. Student practice in these skills comes through classroom activities that require higher-order thinking and affective involvement. These activities involve experiential learning that aligns curriculum, instruction, and assessment as closely as possible. In effect, the classroom is used as a microcosm of the global world. What is learned in the classroom about multicultural and global concepts is constantly applied there as well as in the world beyond.

Think and Act

- How have you dealt with discriminatory comments or jokes in the past?
- What part of your class rules deals with co-responsibility to overcome discrimination of any kind? How is that made clear to the students?
- What does taking a passive role in solving multicultural and global problems imply?

Conclusion

Certain implications for classroom practices can be drawn from the definitions and concepts given in this chapter. Preservice teachers and practicing teachers who have truly understood and adopted multicultural and global concepts should demonstrate these qualities in all that they do as professionals and as caring people. They should apply these concepts in all interactions with their students. They should apply these concepts to the curriculum, texts, materials, and supplementary resources. They should apply these concepts to the teaching strategies and activities for the students. They should apply these concepts in evaluation methods of student achievement. They should apply these concepts in the classroom environment, both physical and emotional/social. These teachers should apply these concepts in the school context. Finally, these teachers should apply multicultural and global concepts in all their interactions in their communities—local, national, and international. Overall, in all the decisions and actions teachers make in their classrooms and communities, teachers themselves must act as role models for the application of multicultural and global concepts.

PART TWO
Applying Multicultural and Global Concepts in the Classroom

The classroom setting for teaching and learning is composed of six critical elements: teacher, students, environment, curriculum, instruction, and assessment. If any of these is altered, the teaching-learning situation is changed. An effective teacher regularly reflects on ways each of these elements and the interactions among them can be addressed to improve student learning. An effective teacher with awareness of multicultural and global concepts includes these concepts in the reflective thinking process.

Because of the tremendous influence a teacher has over what happens in the classroom, the first element to be analyzed is the teacher. The teacher's beliefs, values, attitudes, and assumptions influence teacher and student behavior and help to determine the teaching and learning that takes place. When examining multicultural and global concept application, therefore, starting with teachers and what they bring to their classrooms seems logical.

The second critical classroom element, the students, is equally as important if not more so because learners are at the heart of any teaching-learning situation. Teaching without knowing and understanding the students being taught can rarely if ever be good teaching. Good teaching implies solid learning by all students, and such learning does not happen when the heritages, experiences, interests, and needs of the individual students are not taken into account. After gaining a thorough understanding of themselves, effective teachers try to learn as much as possible about their students. The last four elements—environment, curriculum, instruction, and assessment—play important roles as they interact with the teacher, the students, and each other in the classroom.

In this booklet, the six critical classroom elements are only introduced. For a fuller discussion of applying multicultural and global concepts related to each element, the reader is advised to consult the complete text by Brown and Kysilka (2002).

The Teacher

An investigation of one's own personal beliefs, values, assumptions, and attitudes is a necessary first step towards applying multicultural and global concepts in the classroom. All teachers enter the teaching profession with beliefs, values, assumptions, and attitudes about teaching, learning, and education. Some of these relate directly to the classroom, such as how a "good teacher" should act. Others might be less obvious but still have an influence on the teacher. Religious beliefs, for instance, might not be part of the state-mandated or district-interpreted curriculum. Yet they certainly will have an influence on the curriculum delivered by the teacher and on the hidden curriculum, the part of the curriculum implied by each teacher's attitudes and actions in the classroom and by the school's culture.

Beliefs and values come from each person's unique experiences interpreted and reinterpreted over time. Getting back to those experiences, both external and internal, requires time-consuming and sometimes painful analysis and reflection. External experiences can be seen as interactions with people, things, and events. Internal experiences relate to inner understandings of these interactions and the schemata or relationships the mind and memory make of them. Powerful experiences, those involving deep emotions, leave memories that can be triggered any number of ways. Religious beliefs and values particularly are deep-seated in a combination of personal, family, community, and cultural experiences that contain high emotional impact. Because of the increased emotional pressures on individuals and families during religious holidays, unusually high incidents of violence, even suicide and murder, accompany charity and good will.

Assumptions and attitudes are closely tied to personal beliefs and values in that they are the interpretations of interactions with people, things, and events based on those personal beliefs or values. Teachers make necessary assumptions daily that help them manage their professional world. The difficulty comes not in an action itself but in the interpretation of the action by different individuals. For any college instructor to believe, for instance, that every student attending an education class was there because the course was so fascinating that no one wanted to miss it is foolhardy. Likewise, it would be inappropriate to assume that every student was there because the course was required, not because there was something worthwhile to be learned in class activities.

Like assumptions, attitudes are often unthinking responses in the present based on experiences in the past, but they involve the emotions. Time and again women in elementary education programs report that they do not like and cannot do mathematics. When asked about their negative attitudes toward mathematics, they often report specific incidents either in elementary or high school where they were made to feel mathematically stupid or incompetent. Studies about girls in school support this finding about gender biases, especially in connection with mathematics and science (Sadler & Sadler, 1994; Wellesley College Center for Research on Women, 1992). These preservice elementary teachers have developed negative attitudes based on emotionally charged past experiences. The attitudes and emotions remain to influence consciously and unconsciously present and future teaching and learning situations.

Readers are urged to use a variety of metacognitive techniques to examine their own beliefs, values, assumptions, and attitudes. Dialogue and debate offer chances for verbal interchanges and challenges of other perspectives. Reading and responding to books and articles about multicultural and global issues allow for a more solitary time for reflection and articulation. A personal journal in addition to a professional notebook provides a place for thoughts and feelings too sensitive to share with others. Emotional struggles can be recorded in the journal as a way of releasing the tension and of distancing oneself in order to examine the issue as critically and objectively as possible. Professional decisions resulting from such examinations can then be recorded in the notebook. Exercises investigating cultural heritages and influences provide another way to look at individual beliefs, values, assumptions, and attitudes.

Progress with self-assessment in this critical classroom element of teacher is also progress that will affect all the other elements. As the other five critical classroom elements of students, environment, curriculum, instruction, and assessment are briefly introduced, returning to think about this first critical element will be beneficial in emphasizing the process component of applying multicultural and global education. Preservice and practicing teachers must constantly remind themselves of their beliefs and values, their assumptions and attitudes that must be modified if they expect their students to do likewise.

The Students

One of the essential multicultural and global concepts mentioned earlier is that diversity enriches the world of the classroom and the world outside. The wide variety of students' cultural backgrounds, experiences, knowledge, and beliefs offers every classroom a great richness to be shared. Yet many teachers, either not knowing or not caring, daily ignore this wealth. Teachers who say that they care about their students too often show in their attitudes and their actions that they care only about certain aspects of their students, not the whole unique person.

Once teachers become aware of their own cultural influences, they need to think of how their students' cultural influences differ from theirs and from each other's. Searching for ways to honor these differences within the classroom then becomes a major goal of any teacher applying multicultural and global concepts. This goal entails the understanding of what accommodations must be made for successful learning to take place and who must make those accommodations. Typically, students from diverse backgrounds are pressured by individuals and institutions to become acculturated to the dominant group in order to benefit from a U.S. public school education. Nieto (2000) suggests, however, that students should not be forced to do all the accommodating. Instead, she calls for a negotiation among students, families, teachers, and schools that will create a more equitable teaching and learning environment.

Thus teachers need to look more closely at their students from a variety of perspectives so that they can, by adjusting to and building on student differences, become more effective teachers. First, the examining cultural heritages and influences from the students' perspectives helps provide needed background about the learners. Then exploring a wide variety of student learning styles compared with one's own preferred teaching styles offers more information. Finally, examining cultural learning styles, orientations, and communication styles while avoiding cultural stereotyping leads to other ways to reach all students.

As teachers become more aware and sensitive to individual and group styles and the resulting behaviors, they can build better bridges between the dominant school culture and the various diverse cultures within the classroom. Acting as interpreters, they can explain student behaviors to other students and colleagues.

They can also better explain their own behaviors to students. They, in effect, help all members of the classroom to understand and celebrate diverse ways of perceiving, communicating, and learning.

To act as mediators, preservice and practicing teachers need first to cross over cultural gaps themselves. This is done by adapting personal and professional behaviors to fit the cultural needs of individual students, especially those whose cultural influences are different from the teachers. Next, teachers can act as scaffolding to help students cross over cultural gaps, too. Such mentoring requires teacher sensitivity and solid teacher-student relationships.

Important elements in bridging cultural gaps are teacher awareness of and empathy for students' struggles with cultural conflicts. As students attempt to adjust to the dominant cultural climate of U.S. classrooms, they might encounter difficulties at home. Angie, a Vietnamese student, mentioned the tug of war between school and home. Her mother expected her to maintain the more restrictive daughter role while she was anxious to become the U.S. image of a popular girl. The more she succeeded in school socially, the harder she found her mother's restrictions. Although Angie achieved her goal of success in school with excellent grades and an active social life, the cost of living in two worlds was high. Having teachers who understood what she was going through helped her realize she was not alone in her bicultural balancing struggle (Brown, personal interview, 2000).

All students must have access to the European American middle-class culture in order to take advantage of political, economic, and social possibilities in the United States. Although students are exposed to the dominant culture daily, many do not learn the ways of thinking and behaving easily. Others, like Angie, make sacrifices at home for successes in school. The goal for students should not be assimilation at the cost of their cultural heritages but an ability to live in two or more cultural worlds comfortably. Students of color, students with limited English proficiency, and students in poverty particularly have little hope of accomplishing this demanding flexibility without assistance from knowledgeable and empathetic individuals. Teachers, with thousands of personal interactions with students daily, must be the key mediators. Their awesome power requires them to accept the responsibility of mediating and navigating the diverse cultures within their classrooms.

The Environment

When teachers think of the environment of their students and how it has influenced them, their thoughts usually center upon the home and community outside the school. Too often, these thoughts are negative ones—what the outside environment has not done to prepare the students for school or what it is doing to prevent the students from learning in school. Although they may have little or no influence over some aspects of the outside environment, teachers have a major responsibility for the classroom and school environments that surround students for so much of their childhood and youth.

Like the five other critical elements in the classroom, the environment is complex because it involves a good deal more than the academic side of teaching and learning. The physical, emotional, and social components play a large role in the total well-being of students. Teachers applying multicultural and global concepts to their classroom should consider the six concepts described earlier when analyzing their own unique environment. The classroom environment must celebrate diversity, honor human rights, teach multiple perspectives, develop interconnectedness and interdependence, practice co-responsibility, and experience the global society. Co-ownership and co-responsibility of the physical arrangement and condition as well as the emotional and social climate of the classroom are essential for developing knowledge, skills, attitudes, and behaviors needed in a cooperative and collaborative classroom.

The classroom environment, through its physical appearance and its emotional and social climate, influences all that goes on within the classroom. By being proactive about the desired qualities of the classroom environment, teachers can work with students to establish a healthy learning community in face of even the most discouraging outside-the-classroom environment. Making the physical environment look as warm and welcoming as possible can be the first step. The physical appearance, however, is not as important as the emotional and social climate. Teachers and students alike have the responsibility to make sure everyone is a welcome member of the community. Ongoing vigilance of verbal and nonverbal behavior by teachers and students is needed to establish and maintain positive interpersonal relationships. Key to successful relationships are the twin concepts of self-respect and respect of others. Much of the positive climate can be built through continuing emphasis on the interconnectedness and interdependence of the community members.

The Curriculum

Teachers' personal views of curriculum greatly influence their participation in curriculum development. If teachers view curriculum solely as the state and district written requirements, then the likelihood of their creating or even modifying curriculum becomes diminished. If, however, teachers see curriculum as organic and evolving, then in all probability they will become involved in the process of curriculum development in their classroom. Further, if they see curriculum as a social construction, as developed by individuals and groups according to their goals and objectives, then they will try to involve other stakeholders, particularly their students, in the curriculum development process.

This chapter looks at how the curriculum can be made to reflect multicultural and global concepts and perspectives.

The work of curriculum development is by no means easy. Teachers who have been involved in the active construction of a curriculum know how time-consuming and mind-boggling the planning can be. For issues related to multicultural and global education, the effort is even more frustrating because these fields are filled with controversy. Every cultural category has strong advocates for a variety of stances, whether the category is a seemingly sensitive area such as race or sexual orientation or a less obvious one such as age. Furthermore, multicultural and global education materials are not always of good quality and sometimes are biased or factually inaccurate. Individual teachers, then, are left with the responsibility to sort through the quantities of materials available in order to build a culturally relevant curriculum.

Teachers who wish to incorporate multicultural education into their curriculum might center on ethnic and racial differences or emphasize only personal discrimination rather than institutional problems. These issues are important, especially in secondary schools where racist behaviors by students often become more blatant. Yet emphasizing only ethnic and racial issues and dealing only with the personal aspects ignore the many other areas of multicultural education, such as classism and sexism, and the way institutional discrimination and oppression affect us all. The deep - understandings come from thorough exploration and application of multicultural concepts.

In a similar way, teachers might present a limited view of global education to their students. Lessons might focus on the easier, more obvious problems such as the need to recycle without attacking deep underlying causes such as an economy built on excessive consumerism and the uneven distribution of wealth and resources. Teachers might not understand the need to explore the many aspects of complex issues, but simplifying issues often leaves students with incomplete or inaccurate understandings. For instance, while protesting against shoe companies exploiting child labor in developing countries, students are often not aware of the extreme poverty in those countries and the need for all family members to work to stave off starvation. Even if they understand that, they sometimes do not see the intricate connections between global competition, cheap labor, profit for investors, and relationship to the students' own consumption patterns.

Teachers have a great deal of influence over the curriculum that they teach. Even with numerous state and local restraints, teacher decisions determine exactly what content is taught to students. Teachers applying multicultural and global concepts in their classrooms will concern themselves with all aspects of curriculum development. They will work to change their present curriculum, analyzing the content with the goals of curriculum transformation and social action in mind. They will investigate new content that directly teaches multicultural and global concepts. Teachers also will analyze all curriculum materials for appropriate content and concepts. They will seek out new sources of curriculum materials, including human resources in the community. Finally, they will research their own classroom context, checking to see that the hidden curriculum supports multicultural and global perspectives.

The Instruction

Information about the brain and how an individual learns is exploding in this challenging time of MRIs, CAT scans, and computers. The exciting research and its implications for education include learning styles, multiple intelligences, right and left brain theory, and the like. Learning styles and related areas of information processing are directly linked to instructional strategies, since the teacher's choice of strategy provides the method by which students are expected to learn the content.

Instructional strategies and learning styles are also related to multicultural and global education. Cultural influences on a person might affect his or her learning style, while individual characteristics might reinforce or counteract those cultural influences. Past experiences and present needs and interests influence how the learner and the teacher view the content. Effective teachers use instructional strategies to tap into their learners' experiences, needs, and interests. Effective teachers are also aware of their own preferred teaching styles and recognize how these preferences can hinder learning in their classrooms. Thus, effective teachers work hard to employ a variety of strategies to facilitate learning so that all students have opportunities to succeed in the classroom.

Multicultural and global concepts fit well with constructivist theory. Teachers who use a constructivist approach to instruction are already applying many of the concepts. Constructivist theory sees each individual as the maker of his or her own knowledge (Brooks & Brooks, 1993; Fosnot, 1996). The honoring of the individual learner's attempts to make sense of the information presented is also the honoring of that individual, a basic multicultural and global concept (Mathison & Young, 1995). -Included in recognizing the individual is deliberately bringing the student's prior experiences, cultural heritage, and learning styles as well as present needs into teaching-learning situations. Participation of the learner with other learners, exchanging ideas and viewpoints, supports constructivist theory of dialogue and the multiple perspectives concept. Thus the exploration of individual interests and needs through experience, dialogue, and reflection fits both constructivist theory and multicultural and global education philosophy (Brown, Kysilka, & Warner, 1996).

Teachers can support multicultural and global concepts by the choices they make for instructional strategies. Diversity in the classroom is honored when teachers use a wide variety of instructional strategies to provide for the diverse learning styles of their students. Human rights are honored by giving students autonomy and responsibility through choices of ways to learn. Multiple perspectives are also honored when teachers show and allow many approaches to the same questions or problems. Interconnectedness and interdependence are developed whenever strategies such as cooperative learning are used in the classroom. Co-responsibility is practiced when students help each other to share, work, and learn as a community. Teachers and students together make their classroom a global society when instruction calls for the use of multicultural and global knowledge, skills, attitudes, and behaviors.

The Assessment

The sixth critical element in the classroom is assessment. Classroom assessment covers a wide range of processes by which information is gathered about student learning. Caring teachers look for assessments that will fairly evaluate what their students know and can do. Fairness includes offering students many opportunities to demonstrate their learning, from standardized and teacher-made tests to portfolios and performances. Using a wide variety of assessment methods before, during, and after instructional units helps teachers gain a more comprehensive picture of student learning throughout the learning cycle. This information can then be used to modify curriculum and instruction as well as inform students and parents of progress and achievement. Teachers who are aware of multicultural and global concepts will also be concerned about equity issues such as whether certain types of assessment favor certain types of learners.

Traditional assessment methods have been described as paper-and-pencil tests that depend to a large extent upon verbal-linguistic and/or mathematical-logical abilities. Because they are quick momentary glimpses of student learning, they have been called snapshots of students' learning. Traditional methods usually assess only discrete bits of factual information that have been memorized and reproduced on demand. They do not gauge an individual's ability to apply what has been learned to new and challenging situations so much of the learning is forgotten after the tests (Darling-Hammond, 1991; Wiggins, 1992).

In contrast to traditional assessment methods are methods that have been recently labeled authentic. According to the literature (Montgomery, 2001; Newmann, 1995), what makes an assessment authentic are the following criteria:

1. The assessment is related to real-world tasks.
2. The assessment is complex, involving process, progress, and product.
3. The assessment involves self-assessment by the learner.

Rather than the snapshots of traditional methods, these are seen as moving pictures over time.

Authentic assessment methods better complement multicultural and global concepts because the criteria allow for diversity of learning styles and abilities. Further, the methods are an integral part of the instructional unit so that students can self-assess as they work, thus taking better control of their own learning. Yet few teachers would wish to do away completely with traditional assessment methods. Just as using a variety of instructional strategies benefits students with diverse learning styles, so does using a variety of assessment methods. Teachers need to analyze how they can help students succeed with all types of assessment. First and foremost, assessment for the effective teacher applying multicultural and global concepts is a means of finding out about students' learning in order to help them learn better. As Tomlinson (1999, p. 11) states it, "Assessment always has more to do with helping students grow than with cataloging their mistakes."

Teachers can support multicultural and global concepts by the choices they make for assessment. Recognizing that the dependence on paper-and-pencil tests for assessing student learning will benefit certain students and penalize others is the first step. Using a wide variety of assessment methods in the classroom to give all students a better opportunity of showing what they have learned becomes the next step. Including students in their own assessment throughout the process of learning is a relatively new direction for many teachers. The end result is that students can begin to take more responsibility for their own learning since they participated in the decision-making process along the way. Shared decision making and shared assessment results particularly demonstrate the concept of practicing co-responsibility in the classroom.

PART THREE
Applying Multicultural and Global Concepts Beyond the Classroom

However teachers hope and plan to apply multicultural and global concepts in their classrooms, their decisions are also impacted by outside factors beyond those classrooms. Two major influencing factors are the school beyond the classroom and the communities beyond the school, nearby and farther away. The next part examines these larger arenas and how they can influence—and be influenced by—teachers and their classrooms.

The organization and the operation of the school reflect the beliefs, values, assumptions, and attitudes of its leadership, combined with major influences from teachers, staff, students, parents, and the community the school serves. The community also has its structure and operation reflecting the beliefs, values, assumptions, and attitudes of the parents, community leaders, and other local and regional stakeholders. Sometimes the interests and goals of the school and the community are similar; other times, they are distinctly different. Both entities, in turn, are influenced by the larger communities of region, state, nation, and world. All these influences must be analyzed and incorporated into any action plan for the application of multicultural and global concepts.

The role of the school has been changing and evolving over the past few decades. It is no longer—if it ever really was—an isolated place removed from outside influences. In fact, faculty and administration in effective schools today bring in many forms of outside involvement from reading volunteers to business sponsorship. What teachers and others in the school do to encourage or discourage others has a tremendous effect on the teaching and learning that go on in the classrooms. Chapter 8 examines the school and its components in relationship to the application of multicultural and global concepts.

The roles of local and more distant communities regarding schools are also rapidly changing. New forms of communication have brought the classrooms and schools into instant contact with people and places around the world. Instant electronic contact has led to more interconnections near and far. Politics, for instance, has become more important to schools as district, state, and national groups demand increasing accountability for educational funding. Social, cultural, and economic aspects of these expanding communities are also more intertwined with schools. Effective teachers cannot afford to ignore these varied and complex influences because of the many riches as well as the complications and sometimes even dangers they pose to teaching and learning.

In this booklet, the school and community are only introduced. For a fuller discussion of applying multicultural and global applications in the school and community, the reader is advised to consult the complete text by Brown and Kysilka (2002).

The School

Each school in the United States develops its own culture. This culture is highly influenced by the leadership of the school, by the influence parents may have on that leadership, and by the community that school serves. However, if a school is going to adequately serve the community in which it is located, then the leadership of that school must work hard to develop a culture that is open and accepting of the constituents it serves. In addition, the whole purpose of public education in the United States must not be lost in a school's attempt to gain an identity. According to John Dewey (1916) education has both democratic and societal goals. In order for schools to serve society and to promote democratic principles, they must be organized to reflect the different interests held by the individuals and groups who inhabit the school. Democratic ways of knowing can be taught in the schools if the schools themselves function in democratic ways. Society can become more understanding and supportive of diversity and differences if schools foster those goals. Geneva Gay (1994) says it well, "Creating a cohesive society out of this country's incredible diversity requires knowledge, skills and values that can, and should, be taught" (p. 93).

According to Jerome Bruner (1996), "culture in a macro sense is a system of values, rights, exchanges, obligations, opportunities and power" and in the micro sense "it examines how the demands of the `macro' affects those who must operate within it; how the individual makes meaning out of experiences" (p. 11). School culture (micro) is often a reflection of the larger community culture (macro), and thus what happens within the environment of the school is what the students assume will happen within the broader context of society. Consequently, it is imperative that the school culture or environment is a positive, open, accepting one that models what should be in the broader social, economic, and political culture of society. Schools must not only be a reflection of, but should be a change agent for, a more pluralistic, global, tolerant, positive society.

All members of a school contribute to its character as a center for learning. Who gets recognized and who gets marginalized depend very much upon the complex interactions and interconnectedness of administrators, faculty, staff, and students. Explicit decisions such as what extracurricular programs are supported and implicit decisions such as what privileges are given to sports stars contribute to the composite picture of a school and its culture. Many schools today have mission and vision statements. Whether a school actually lives up to these ideals depends upon the individuals and groups within it.

The Community

The application of multicultural and global concepts within classrooms and schools cannot be adequately addressed by teachers unless they also understand how these same issues and concerns relate to the communities where the schools are located. What makes multicultural and global concepts imperative for every classroom also affects each community and how it views its schools.

In the past decades many communities have faced changing demographics. Population changes might be related to increasing numbers of immigrants, particularly Latinos, Asians and Pacific Islanders, and Eastern Europeans. Changes could also been related to economic shifts, as industries particularly in the North continue to downsize while companies in the Sunbelt regions are established or expanded. Areas such as the Silicon Valley have seen such phenomenal growth that the cost of living has skyrocketed, driving out working class and poor families. Whatever the reason, the population in the United States has shown many shifts and new trends over the past few decades.

These changing demographics and the resultant interests and needs of each community are reflected in the ways schools are viewed and operated. Changing demographics, increased interaction among cultural groups, the interconnectedness and interdependence of all participants in the local and the global village—these concerns and many others are part of everyday life in even the most isolated U.S. community.

Teachers must be seen by the community as responsible adults who are working to improve educational opportunities of all children. They do not deserve to be treated as second-class citizens by the parents or community leaders. Their opinions and ideas should be valued, not dismissed. To create positive impressions and change negative ones, teachers have to be intimately involved in the decision making about what happens in schools and to students. Schools, according to Sarason (1990) "must be coequally accommodating to the development of teachers and students" (pp. 146–147). Consequently, how teachers interact with community members becomes very important.

Since demographics strongly impact schools, it is imperative for school personnel to study the demographics of their community. Knowledge of who is in the community can help teachers and administrators understand what they need to do to meet the needs of all their students along with serving the interests of the community.

Teachers have wonderful resources available in their local communities and beyond. Working with individuals and groups to develop these resources can be time-consuming, but the rewards are well worth the effort. Teachers and schools can no longer afford to be isolated from their local and greater communities. The world of today reaches into the classroom even if the teacher has tried to close the door. Effective teachers realize the importance of allies in educating their students. They understand that they alone cannot possibly provide all the resources and information necessary to lead their students toward active participation in the local and global societies. In this information age, collaboration is vital.

REFERENCES

Ahlquist, R. (1992). Manifestations of inequality: Overcoming resistance in a multicultural foundations course. In C. Grant (Ed.), Research and multicultural education: From the margins to the mainstream (pp. 89–105). London: Falmer.

Banks, J. A. (1991). Teaching strategies for ethnic studies. Boston: Allyn and Bacon.

———. (1994). Multiethnic education: Theory and practice (3rd ed.). Boston: Allyn and Bacon.

———. (1997). Educating citizens in a multicultural society. New York: Teachers College Press.

Brooks, J., & Brooks, M. (1993). In search of understanding: The case for constructivist classrooms. Alexandria, VA: Association for Supervision and Curriculum Development.

Brown, S. C. (1993). Application of multicultural and global concepts in senior elementary interns' classrooms. Unpublished doctoral dissertation, University of Central Florida, Orlando.

Brown, S. C. & Kysilka, M. L. (2002). Applying multicultural and global concepts to the classroom and beyond. Boston: Allyn and Bacon.

Brown, S. C., Kysilka, M. L., & Warner, M. J. (1996). Applying constructivist theory to multicultural education content. In M. Kompf, R. Bond, D. Dworet, & R. T. Boak (Eds.), Changing research and practice: Teachers' professionalism, identities and knowledge (pp. 167–174). Washington, DC: Falmer Press.

Bruner, J. (1996). The culture of education. Cambridge, MA: Harvard University Press.

Cole, D. J. (1984, Spring). Multicultural education and global education: A possible merger. Theory into Practice, 23(2), 151–154.

Darling-Hammond, L. (1991). The implications of testing policy for quality and equity. Phi Delta Kappan, 73(3): 220–225.

de Anda, D. (1997). Controversial issues in multiculturalism. Boston: Allyn and Bacon.

Delpit, L. (1995). Other people's children: Cultural conflict in the classroom. New York: The New Press.

Dewey, J. (1916). Democracy and education: An introduction to the philosophy of education. New York: Macmillan.

Diaz, C. F., Massialas, B. G., & Xanthopoulos, J. A. (1999). Global perspectives for educators. Boston: Allyn and Bacon.

Fosnot, C. T. (Ed.). (1996). Constructivism: Theory, perspectives, and practice. New York: Teachers College Press.

Freire, P. (1998). Teachers as cultural workers: Letters to those who dare to teach. Boulder, CO: Westview Press.

Gay, G. (1994). At the essence of learning: Multicultural education. West Lafayette, IN: Kappa Delta Pi.

Giroux, H. A. (1996). Fugitive cultures: race, violence, and youth. New York: Routledge.

Gregersen, H. B., & Black, J. S. (1990). A multifaceted approach to expatriate retention in international assignments. Group and Organization Studies, 15(4): 461–485.

Hall, P. H., & Gudykunst, W. B. (1989). The relationship of perceived ethnocentrisim in corporate cultures to the selection, training, and success of international employees. International Journal of Intercultural Relations, 13: 183–201.

Hanvey, R. (1976). An attainable global perspective. Denver, CO: Center for Teaching International Relations.

Howard, G. (1999). We can't teach what we don't know: White teachers, multicultural schools. New York: Teachers College Press.

Kirkwood, T. F. (1990). Global education as an agent for school change. In K. A. Tye (Ed.), Global education: From thought to action (pp. 142–56). Alexandria, VA: Association for Supervision and Curriculum Development.

Kniep, W. (1986). Defining a global education by its content. Social Education, 50(10): 437–66.

Kozol, J. (1991). Savage inequalities: Children in America's schools. New York: Crown.

Lynch, J. (1992). Education for citizenship in a multicultural society. London, England: Cassell.

Mathison, C., & Young, R. (1995). Constructivism and multicultural education: A mighty pedagogical merger. Multicultural Education, 2(4): 7–11.

Merryfield, M. (1994). Teacher education in global and international education. Washington, DC: American Association of Colleges for Teacher Education.

Merryfield, M. M., Jarchow, E., & Pickert, S. (Eds.). (1997). Preparing teachers to teach global perspectives. Thousand Oaks, CA: Corwin Press.

Montgomery, K. (2001). Authentic assessment: A guide for elementary teachers. New York: Longman.

National Council for the Social Studies (NCSS). (1982). Position statement on global education. Washington, DC: Author.

Newmann, F. M. (1995). Authentic pedagogy: Standards that boost student performance. (ERIC Document Reproduction Service No. ED 390 906)

Nieto, S. (2000). Affirming diversity: The sociopolitical context of multicultural education (3rd ed.). New York: Longman.

Ravitch, D. (1990). Multiculturalism: E pluribus plures. The American Scholar, 59(3): 337–354.

Sadler, M., & Sadler, D. (1994). Failing at fairness: How our schools cheat girls. New York: Simon & Schuster.

Santrock, J. W. (1997). Life-span development (7th ed.). Boston: McGraw Hill.

———. (2001). Adolescence (8th ed.). Boston: McGraw Hill.

Sarason, S. (1990). The predictable failure of educational reform. San Francisco, CA: Jossey-Bass.

Sleeter, C., & Grant, C. (1988). Making choices for multicultural education: Five approaches to race, class, and gender. Columbus, OH: Merrill.

Sleeter, C. E., & McLaren, P. L. (1995). Introduction: Exploring connections to build a critical multiculturalism. In C. E. Sleeter & P. L. McLaren (Eds.), Multicultural education, critical pedagogy, and the politics of difference (pp. 5–32). Albany: State University of New York.

Tomlinson, C. A. (1999). The differentiated classroom: Responding to the needs of all learners. Alexandria, VA: Association for Supervision and Curriculum Development.

Wellesley Center for Research on Women. (1992). How schools shortchange girls. Washington, DC: American Association of University Women Educational Foundation.

Wiggins, G. (1992). Creating tests worth taking. Educational Leadership, 49(8): 26–33.